The Junior Gourmet

I dedicate this book to my family; my parents, Pat and David
Long, and Uncle Ian Long, who have unconditionally supported
and encouraged my love of food, cooking and travel.

— *E.L.*

Recipe acknowledgements: *Michael Lambie, Jane Webster, Sarah Mountford,
Chris Ong, Kris Sharples, Justin Hays, Beryl Long, Barry Iddles, Maria Teresa
Peirano, Gargi Nihit Patel, Aunty Anne, Gail Roche, Jacqui Roche*

The Five Mile Press Pty Ltd
1 Centre Road, Scoresby
Victoria 3179 Australia
www.fivemile.com.au

Photography by Julie Renouf
Food styling by Cherise Pagano
Illustrations by Jane Newham
Design by Kristy Lund-White
All other images courtesy of Shutterstock

Catalogue-in-Publication data available from the National Library of Australia

The Junior Gourmet

AMAZING RECIPES FROM AROUND THE WORLD

ELIZABETH LONG

The Five Mile Press

Contents

Introduction

G'day, salut, ciao, hola, preevyet, xin chao!

Welcome to a cookbook that will take you and your tastebuds on a journey around the world! Explore the amazing cultures and cuisines of places as diverse as Mexico and Morocco, and learn how to cook delicious, simple recipes that will be sure to impress your family and friends.

Here is a simple checklist to make sure each recipe is a success:

- Plan and write down your shopping list for all ingredients.
- Ensure you have all the equipment you need before you begin.
- Make sure you have allowed enough time to cook the recipe.
- Ask a parent or adult to help you with the tricky steps.
- Read the recipe through carefully before starting to cook.
- If your recipe requires oven cooking, don't forget to pre-heat your oven.
- Clean up as you go.
- Make sure you taste your cooking before adding additional seasoning.
- Make sure you have a plate or platter ready to serve your dish.
- Have fun and always be proud of what you have cooked!

Always remember, cooking can be an experiment – you may decide to leave a spice out of a recipe, or to add a little more or less to taste – that's okay. Maybe you would prefer to substitute chicken for lamb, or even make the recipe vegetarian – try it and see! Some recipes, such as cakes and pastries, usually need to be followed closely, but others can be more flexible. You may find that you create a brand new delicious dish all of your own.

Fabulous food is all about the time and the love you put into each recipe, so don't forget to share your cooking with family and friends.

Have fun exploring these amazing dishes from around the world!

ELIZABETH LONG

Kitchen techniques

COOKING PASTA

Ensure your pot is big enough for the amount of pasta you will be cooking. Once the water has come to a rapid boil, add a couple of pinches of salt and a tablespoon of olive oil. Pasta should be cooked *al dente*, which is to the 'tooth' – still slightly firm in the centre, and not too soft or squishy.

SEPARATING EGGS

Crack your egg lightly on the edge of a cup or bowl, splitting the shell in two. Turn the shell upright, keeping the yolk in the lower half of the shell. Let the egg white dribble into the cup, keeping the yolk in the half shell. When all the egg white has been removed, place the yolk into another cup.

DE-VEINING PRAWNS

Remove the head of the prawn by giving it a quick twist. Take the legs of the prawn and pull the shell away from the body. Take a skewer and insert it just behind the head, and then draw the whole vein out slowly.

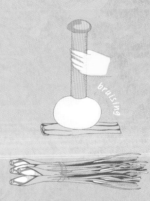

CLEANING AND DE-BEARDING MUSSELS

Ensure you scrub each mussel shell to remove any stringy bits. The beard looks like little threads of seaweed sticking out of one side of the shell. Take hold of the beard and give it a gentle tug, side to side, until it slides out.

CRUSHING GARLIC

Take a knife and place it flat over an unpeeled clove. Press down with some force – the skin of the garlic clove should split, and the skin can then be removed easily. Sprinkle a little sea salt over the garlic clove, and chop finely. You can also purchase a special garlic crusher to make this job easier.

BRUISING LEMONGRASS

Remove the spiky end and the root end of the lemongrass with a knife. Then remove the outer layers and discard. Take a pestle, meat mallet or cleaver, and hit the lemongrass a few times. This will release the aroma and flavour into your cooking.

zesting

crushing

GRATING ZEST

You can use a zester or grater to shave thin pieces of skin from oranges, lemons or limes. It is important to only use the zest (the outer skin) and not the pith (the white part under the skin), as the zest will add lovely flavours to your cooking, but the pith will be bitter.

AROMATIC FRYING

The first step in making many soups, sauces and curries is to fry the herbs or spices in a little oil. This will start to release the flavour and aroma of these ingredients.

USING A MORTAR AND PESTLE

A mortar and pestle is great for grinding fresh herbs into a paste, and for crushing and blending spices. Always ensure your mortar and pestle are clean before use, and use a crushing motion rather than pounding.

DEGLAZING

A tasty sauce can be made by first loosening the browned pieces of food that have stuck to a pan or roasting tray. Use either stock or wine over a medium high heat.

STIR-FRYING

Is a Chinese cooking technique that has been adopted by many other cuisines. Meat, fish and vegetables are cut up into small pieces and fried quickly over a high heat, usually in a special frypan called a wok.

PROVING DOUGH

Activating the yeast is a very important step when making bread, pizza and donut dough. Place the dough in a large stainless steel bowl and cover tightly with plastic wrap. The dough will then need to sit in a warm place until it has at least doubled in size.

CARAMELISING

You can caramelise onions, sugar, pineapple and many other things. Onions are caramelised by combining finely sliced onions, oil and balsamic vinegar and cooking over a low heat. To caramelise sugar, add sugar and a little water in a saucepan and stir over a low heat until the sugar has dissolved. Turn the heat up until the sugar stock has thickened and become golden brown.

Ingredients

Some of the ingredients called for in
these recipes may not be familiar to you.
Here are just a few that you might need to use.

FRIED SHALLOTS are a common garnish in Asian cooking. They can be bought in all Asian food stores and supermarkets.

RICE VINEGAR is used in Asian cooking. There are black and white rice vinegars, which vary in taste from sweet to sour. Check your recipe for which one to buy.

ATTA FLOUR is used to make Indian flatbreads such as roti and naan. It is made from an Indian wheat crop which is also known as durum wheat.

SMOKED PAPRIKA is a seasoning used in cooking all around the world. It comes in a range of tastes from mild to hot. You can adapt your recipe with your choice of paprika.

SHERRY VINEGAR is a vinegar produced from sherry, however, it has no alcohol content. Sherry vinegar is used to make salad dressings and to enhance the flavours of sauces, soups and casseroles

PALM SUGAR is used in many Thai dishes. It is often sold in a solid disc or block. The easy way to break it down is to 'shave' it using a grater.

KECAP MANIS is a very popular Indonesian soy sauce. It is sweet and syrupy. There are several brands which can be found in most supermarkets or Asian food stores.

FISH SAUCE is used in many Thai, Vietnamese and East Asian cuisines. It has a strong smell, but is a vital ingredient in many dishes.

GELATINE comes in several forms – powder, granules and sheets of different quality and strength. It is used as a setting agent for mousses, pannacottas, marshmallows and jams.

GARAM MASALA is an Indian spice, made up of a number of spices which are mixed, toasted and then ground. There are variations between different regions.

SEA SALT differs from table salt in texture and taste. It is preferable to use sea salt in savoury dishes.

ORANGE BLOSSOM WATER is a Middle Eastern ingredient, which adds a citrus scent to food. It is sold in small bottles, as usually only a few drops are needed. It can be found in Middle Eastern shops and fine-food stores.

BABY RED CHARD is from the Swiss chard family, it is a small leaf that is often used in salads. It has a pink or purple colour and it can be eaten raw or cooked.

YEAST is a key ingredient in most dough, such as bread, donut and pizza bases. There are several different types: fresh yeast works faster than dry yeast but it has a shorter shelf life.

HORSERADISH is a plant root that is used in condiments and sauces. Fresh horseradish is best when grated. The finer it is grated, the more intense the flavour.

SAFFRON is a little thread at the centre of a small purple crocus flower. They are often sold in fine-food stores. Saffron is an essential ingredient in French bouillabaisse, paella, and Indian biryanis.

CRÈME FRAÎCHE is a French sour cream that is typically thicker and less 'sour' than regular sour cream.

POMEGRANATE MOLASSES is an essential ingredient in traditional Middle Eastern cooking. It is made from pomegranate juice, sugar and lemon juice. It is fabulous with salads or drizzled over a dessert.

Australia

has one of the most dynamic and
diverse food cultures in the world.

Indigenous Australians hunted emus, kangaroos, snakes and lizards,
and collected wild berries and many kinds of edible insects. Waves
of migrants have also brought their influences, so combinations of
many different cuisines can be found in Australian cooking.

Barbecued prawns with dill sauce

'Prawns on the barbie' is a classic Australian dish. In this version the prawns are marinated with chilli and garlic – this also works well with calamari or chicken.

Serves: 6

Cooking and preparation time: 50 minutes + 1 hour for marinating

INGREDIENTS

18 large raw prawns, shelled leaving the tails intact, de-veined

2 small red chillies, finely chopped

3 garlic cloves, crushed

1/2 bunch flat-leaf parsley, chopped

3 tablespoons olive oil, plus extra for the barbecue

DILL SAUCE

1 bunch dill, leaves picked

2 tablespoons dijon mustard

2 tablespoons white vinegar

2 tablespoons white sugar

200 ml extra-virgin olive oil

sea salt and freshly ground black pepper

METHOD

1. Combine prawns, chilli, garlic, parsley and oil in a bowl and toss well. Leave to marinate in the refrigerator for 1 hour.

2. To make the sauce: combine the dill, mustard, vinegar and sugar in a blender or food processor and begin processing. Slowly pour in the oil while the motor is running, and season to taste with salt and pepper. Transfer the sauce to a serving bowl.

3. Heat a barbecue plate to high heat. While it is heating, thread the prawns onto skewers with 3 prawns on each. Lightly oil the hot barbecue plate and add the skewered prawns, cooking for around 1 minute on each side. Serve immediately with the dill sauce.

 Tasty witchetty grubs live among the roots of the native witchetty bush in Central Australia. They are high in protein, and were traditionally one of the most important edible insects for Indigenous Australians.

Chocolate lamingtons

Lamingtons are usually made with sponge cake, which is cubed and coated in chocolate icing and coconut. This is an extra-chocolatey version made with chocolate cake.

Makes 25 lamingtons

Cooking and preparation time: 90 minutes

INGREDIENTS

CAKE

520 g (3 ¹/₂ cups) plain flour

750 g (3 ¹/₃ cups) caster sugar

135 g (1 cup) Dutch cocoa

2 teaspoons bicarbonate of soda

4 eggs

120 ml white vinegar

300 ml vegetable oil

70 ml espresso coffee

600 ml milk

ICING

500 g icing sugar

60 g (¹/₂ cup) Dutch cocoa

350 ml hot water

2 cups desiccated coconut

METHOD

1. Preheat the oven to 170°C. Butter a 25 x 36 cm cake tin and line the base and sides with baking paper.

2. Sift the flour, sugar, cocoa and bicarbonate of soda into a large bowl and stir well.

3. Lightly whisk the eggs in a separate bowl, then add the vinegar, oil, coffee and milk and mix well.

4. Pour the liquid ingredients into the dry ingredients and mix until just combined, being careful not to over-mix.

5. Pour the batter into the cake tin and bake in the oven for 40 minutes, or until a skewer comes out clean when inserted into the middle of the cake. Leave the cake to cool in the tin for a few minutes, then transfer to a wire rack and leave to cool completely.

6. To make the icing: combine the icing sugar and cocoa in a bowl and slowly whisk in the hot water, mixing to a smooth, runny sauce.

7. Put the coconut in a separate bowl. Cut the cake into 5 cm squares.

8. Dip the squares in the icing, coating well, then place on a wire rack for a minute or two to allow the excess icing to drip off. Gently roll the squares in coconut and place on a tray. Chill the lamingtons in the refrigerator until the icing is set.

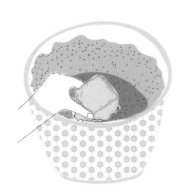

Vietnam

Vietnamese cuisine means fresh flavours, minimal cooking and lots of colour. A family meal is usually made up of a selection of shared dishes – typically a meat or fish, rice, steamed or wok cooked vegetables and dipping sauces.

Chicken noodle salad

You can leave the poached chicken out of this salad to make it vegetarian, or use beef, prawns or just about any other meat or seafood. The salad can also be used as the filling for rice-paper rolls.

Serves: 6

Cooking and preparation time: 90 minutes

INGREDIENTS

250 ml rice vinegar

220 g (1 cup) white sugar

2 carrots, sliced into matchsticks

1 red capsicum, sliced into long thin strips

1 red onion, finely sliced

250 g dried rice-stick noodles

sea salt

6 small chicken breast fillets

1/2 iceberg lettuce or Chinese cabbage (wombok), finely shredded

1 cup roasted peanuts

2 handfuls bean sprouts

1/2 bunch coriander, leaves picked

1/2 bunch mint, leaves picked

1/2 bunch Vietnamese mint, leaves picked

80–100 ml sweet chilli sauce

2–3 teaspoons fish sauce

1/2 cup fried shallots

METHOD

1. Bring the vinegar and sugar to boil in a small saucepan, stirring until the sugar dissolves.

2. Combine the carrot, capsicum and onion in a bowl and pour over the hot vinegar mixture. Set aside to cool, allowing the vegetables to lightly pickle.

3. Put the noodles in a large bowl and cover with plenty of boiling water. Leave for 5 minutes, or until soft, then drain well and return to the bowl.

4. While the noodles are softening, bring a large saucepan of water to boil with several pinches of salt. Add the chicken breast fillets and simmer gently for around 20 minutes, until cooked through (to check, insert the tip of a knife into a thick part of breast to see that flesh is no longer pink). Drain the chicken and leave to rest for 10 minutes before slicing thickly. Add to the bowl of drained noodles.

5. Drain the pickled vegetables, discarding the vinegar, and add to the noodles.

6. Also add the lettuce or cabbage, peanuts, bean sprouts, herbs and sauces (to taste) and toss well.

6. Serve the salad sprinkled with fried shallots.

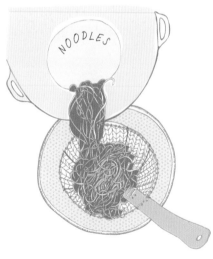

Rice is grown throughout Vietnam. It is used in everyday meals, and can be made into noodles. Rice can also be made into wine!

Crab cakes

These crab cakes make great finger food for a party, or could form a meal if accompanied by a salad. Serve with wedges of lime – or for something more elaborate, you can make a mayonnaise with chilli and coriander.

Makes 15 crab cakes

Cooking and preparation time: 90 minutes

INGREDIENTS

250 g skinless white fish fillet

sea salt

250 g potatoes, peeled and cut into large dice

1 garlic clove, crushed

grated zest of 3 lemons

1 small red chilli, finely chopped

500 g freshly picked crabmeat (or frozen crabmeat)

1/2 bunch Vietnamese mint, finely chopped

1/2 bunch coriander, finely chopped

4 eggs

breadcrumbs

vegetable oil for deep-frying

lime wedges to serve

AROMATIC MILK

500 ml milk

1/2 carrot, finely diced

1/2 celery stalk, finely diced

1/2 onion or leek, finely diced

1/2 lemongrass stalk, bruised

1 garlic clove, bruised

2.5 cm piece of ginger, bruised

1 kaffir lime leaf

1 bay leaf

1 sprig thyme

METHOD

1. Season the fish with salt all over and set aside for 15 minutes.

2. Meanwhile, boil the potatoes until soft. Drain well, then transfer to a large bowl and mash until smooth. Leave to cool.

3. Make the aromatic milk by bringing the milk and other ingredients to boil in a medium saucepan. Remove from the heat and add the fish. Leave the fish in the milk for around 8 minutes, until just cooked through (check by inserting the tip of a small knife into the thickest part of the fish to see that the flesh is no longer translucent). Remove the fish from the milk and leave to cool.

4. Stir the garlic, lemon zest and chilli into the cooled mashed potato. Flake the fish on top, removing any bones, and add the crabmeat and herbs. Stir well and add salt to taste.

5. Put some plain flour in a bowl. Add the eggs to another bowl and beat well with a fork. Put some breadcrumbs in a third bowl.

6. Use your hands to shape the fish and potato mixture into small torpedoes (otherwise known as croquettes). As you finish shaping each one, roll it in flour, dip it in egg, then roll it in breadcrumbs, and set aside on a plate as you continue making croquettes with the rest of the mixture.

7. Pour vegetable oil into a large saucepan to one-third full and place over medium–high heat. Heat to 180°C (if you don't have a thermometer, test the temperature by dropping in a small cube of bread – it should start frying rapidly). Fry the crab cakes in batches for around 3 minutes, until golden brown. Drain on paper towel.

8. Serve the hot crab cakes with lime wedges.

Thailand

Thai cuisine is famous for its use of fresh herbs and spices.

Thai meals often consist of a range of lightly prepared dishes that can be shared among many people. When choosing ingredients, emphasis is placed on a balance of flavours – sweet, salty, sour and spicy.

Egg nets with chicken and prawn

Egg nets are great fun to make as you can use your fingertips to drizzle the egg into the pan. Make them as small or as large as you like.

Serves: 4 mains or 8 entrées

Cooking and preparation time: 45 minutes + 1 hour for refrigeration

INGREDIENTS

4 eggs

vegetable oil

1 lemongrass stalk (white part only), sliced

3 garlic cloves

5 cm piece of ginger, sliced

1 long red chilli, seeded and sliced

2 kaffir lime leaves, finely shredded

4 red shallots, finely sliced

600 g minced chicken

300 g shelled raw prawns, chopped

100 g light palm sugar, shaved

150 ml coconut milk

3 tablespoons fish sauce

250 g bean sprouts

1 cup coriander leaves, roughly chopped, plus extra leaves to garnish

1 cup Vietnamese mint leaves, roughly chopped, plus extra leaves to garnish

2 spring onions, finely sliced

1/2 cup roasted peanuts, roughly chopped

METHOD

1. Crack the eggs into a bowl and beat well with a fork. Strain the mixture through a fine sieve into another bowl and refrigerate for 1 hour, allowing the mixture to settle.

2. Heat a frying pan over medium heat and coat with a little oil. Dip your fingertips into the bowl of beaten egg, then quickly drizzle the egg in a crisscross pattern over the pan to create a net. Once the egg is set, use an egg lifter to lift the net from the pan and slide it onto a plate. Repeat the process with the remaining mixture. Set the nets aside.

3. Use a mortar and pestle to pound the lemongrass, garlic, ginger, chilli and kaffir lime to a paste. Alternatively, use a blender or small food processor.

4. Heat a wok over high heat. Add 1 tablespoon of oil and the shallots and fry for about 1 minute, until golden. Add the lemongrass paste and cook for another minute.

5. Add the minced chicken, stirring constantly to break up the lumps. Cook for 3–5 minutes, until lightly browned, then add the chopped prawns and stir-fry for a further 2 minutes.

6. Add the palm sugar and stir-fry until the mixture begins to caramelise. Add the coconut milk and bring to the boil. Cook for about 3 minutes, allowing the milk to reduce. Remove from the heat and stir through the fish sauce. Allow the mixture to cool slightly.

7. Stir in the bean sprouts, coriander and mint. Spoon some mixture into the centre of each egg net and roll up to enclose the filling.

8. Serve the parcels topped with extra coriander, mint leaves, spring onions and chopped peanuts.

Lemongrass and kaffir lime pannacotta

Pannacotta is a silky mousse-style dessert. It can come in many flavours, such as chocolate or raspberry – this one has Thai flavours of lemongrass and kaffir lime.

Makes 12 pannacottas

Cooking and preparation time: 30 minutes + overnight for refrigeration

INGREDIENTS

5 cardamom pods

6 gelatine sheets

850 ml cream

280 ml milk

140 g white sugar

5 cm piece of lemongrass, bruised

5 kaffir lime leaves

METHOD

1. Put the cardamom pods in a small frying pan and gently toast until aromatic. Tip into a mortar and crush.

2. Soak the gelatine sheets in a bowl of cold water for 5–10 minutes, until soft.

3. Meanwhile, put the cream, milk, sugar, lemongrass, lime leaves and cardamom in a saucepan and bring to the boil, then remove from the heat.

4. Squeeze excess water from the gelatine and stir into the hot cream until dissolved.

5. Place the saucepan inside a large bowl of ice to cool the cream. Once it starts to thicken, strain it into a jug, discarding the aromatics. Pour into small moulds and refrigerate overnight.

6. To help release the pannacottas from the moulds, gently touch the edge of each pannacotta with your finger and carefully draw it away from the side of the mould to create a small air gap. This should allow the pannacottas to slip out of the moulds when you turn them upside down onto plates. If that isn't successful, dip the pannacotta moulds very briefly in hot water and turn onto plates.

cream mixture

Did you know? Fish sauce is used in almost all Thai dishes, adding a distinctive aroma and intense flavour to Thai food. It is made from fermented fish, typically anchovies.

China

Staples in China are rice, noodles and vegetables such as bok choy. Seasoning sauces, such as soy sauce, feature in many dishes. Regional dishes include Beijing (Peking) duck, Cantonese stir fry, and spicy Sichuan food such as Kung Pao chicken.

Pork spring rolls

Spring rolls – perfect at any time of the day! They can be filled with all kinds of meat and vegetable fillings, and should always be served piping hot with a dipping sauce.

Makes 14 spring rolls

Cooking and preparation time: 1 hour + 1 hour for refrigeration

INGREDIENTS

3 tablespoons vegetable oil, plus extra for deep-frying

1 onion, finely diced

1 leek, finely sliced

1 carrot, finely diced

500 g minced pork

1/2 teaspoon ground cumin

1/2 teaspoon freshly ground black pepper

2 teaspoons oyster sauce

1 tablespoon white sugar

3 tablespoons potato flour

14 medium spring roll wrappers

kecap manis (sweet soy sauce) to serve

METHOD

1. Heat 2 tablespoons of the oil in a wok over medium heat and add the onion, leek and carrot. Stir-fry for 5 minutes, or until tender. Add the pork and stir-fry for 5 minutes, breaking up the lumps, until browned. Add the cumin, pepper, oyster sauce, sugar and remaining oil and cook for another 2 minutes.

2. Combine 2 tablespoons of the potato flour with 100 ml of water in a small bowl, then add to the wok. Cook for another minute, stirring until thickened. Transfer the mixture to a bowl and leave to cool slightly before refrigerating for 1 hour to cool thoroughly.

3. Combine the remaining potato flour with 1 tablespoon of water. Lay a spring-roll wrapper on a work surface with one of the corners pointing towards you. Spoon 2 tablespoons of the pork mixture across the centre of the wrapper. Fold the corner that is pointing towards you over the filling, and tuck in the side corners. Roll up the spring roll, brushing the end corner with the flour mixture to stick it down.

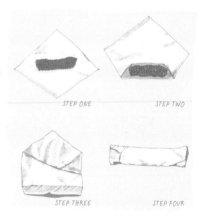

STEP ONE   STEP TWO

STEP THREE   STEP FOUR

4. When you have used all the filling, wipe the wok clean and pour oil into the wok to one-third full. Place over medium–high heat and heat the oil to 180°C (test the temperature by dropping in a small cube of bread – it should start frying rapidly). Fry the spring rolls in 2 batches for around 3 minutes each, until golden brown. Drain on paper towel.

5. Serve immediately with kecap manis for dipping.

Did you know? Yum cha is traditionally a Chinese morning or afternoon meal of dim sum and Chinese tea. Dim sum are a variety of small, hearty dishes that can be steamed or fried, savoury or sweet.

Duck and lychee san choi bao

San choi bao is a dish of flavoursome meat served warm in lettuce cups. The meat can be pork, chicken or duck, either finely chopped or minced. It makes a great lunch or starter.

Serves: 6

Cooking and preparation time: 40 minutes

INGREDIENTS

1 iceberg lettuce

3 tablespoons vegetable oil

2 garlic cloves, finely chopped

2.5 cm piece of ginger, finely chopped

$^1/_2$ red onion, finely chopped

1 celery stalk, finely chopped

8 shiitake mushrooms, soaked in hot water for 30 minutes, squeezed dry and finely chopped

1 roasted duck, meat taken from the bones and finely chopped (including the skin)

2 tablespoons Chinese rice wine

1 tablespoon dark soy sauce

2 tablespoons oyster sauce

1 teaspoon sesame oil

1 teaspoon sugar

pinch of freshly ground white pepper

120 g tinned lychees, diced

$^1/_2$ cup coriander leaves

6 spring onions, finely sliced diagonally

METHOD

1. Soak the lettuce for 30 minutes in cold water. Take from the water and bang a few times on a bench, core-side down. This should help loosen the core. Twist out the core and discard, and carefully peel off each leaf layer by layer. Use scissors to trim the leaves into neat cups and set aside.

2. Heat a wok over high heat until smoking, then add the oil, garlic and ginger. Stir-fry for 20 seconds.

3. Add the onion, celery and mushrooms and stir-fry for a few minutes, then add the duck, rice wine, sauces, sesame oil, sugar and pepper. Toss to heat through, then remove from the heat and stir in the lychees and coriander.

4. To serve, spoon the filling into lettuce cups and garnish with spring onions.

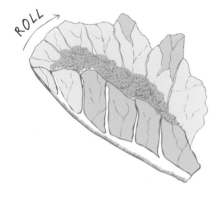

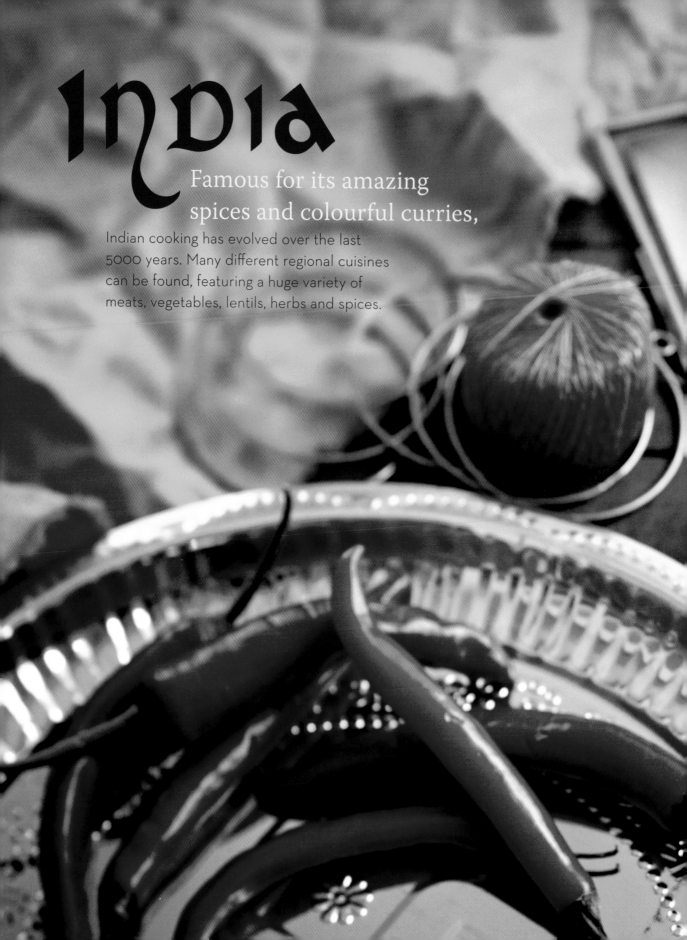

INDIA

Famous for its amazing spices and colourful curries,

Indian cooking has evolved over the last 5000 years. Many different regional cuisines can be found, featuring a huge variety of meats, vegetables, lentils, herbs and spices.

Chicken curry

This mild and tasty curry is perfect with steamed rice and pappadums.
It can also be made with beef, lamb or pork.

Serves: 4–6

**Cooking and preparation
time:** 1 hour + 6 hours for
marinating

INGREDIENTS

2 teaspoons ground cardamom

2 teaspoons turmeric

1 tablespoon garam marsala

2 teaspoons chilli powder

2 teaspoons ground cumin

7.5 cm piece of ginger, grated

3 garlic cloves, crushed

125 ml natural yoghurt

1 tablespoon lemon juice

1 kg chicken breast fillets, cut into
large dice

1 tablespoon vegetable oil

60 g unsalted butter

1 onion, sliced

1 red capsicum, sliced

200 g green beans, topped and tailed

1 medium zucchini, cut into thick
rectangles

400 ml tomato puree

200 ml chicken stock

250 ml cream

1 bay leaf

1 cinnamon stick

sea salt

1 cup coriander leaves

METHOD

1. Mix the dry spices, ginger and garlic in a
   small bowl.

2. Scoop half the mixture into a large bowl
   and stir in the yoghurt and lemon juice.
   Add the chicken and toss well. Cover
   with plastic wrap and leave to marinate
   in the refrigerator for at least 6 hours,
   or overnight. Cover the bowl of
   remaining spices and set aside until
   you are ready to cook the chicken.

Dry spice + yoghurt + lemon juice

3. Heat the oil and butter in a heavy-based pot over medium heat. Add
   the onion and fry for 2 minutes, then turn the heat to low and add the
   remaining spice mixture. Fry gently until aromatic.

4. Add the capsicum, beans and zucchini and cook, stirring, for a further
   2 minutes. Turn the heat up to medium and add the chicken and its
   marinade. Cook, stirring, for 2–3 minutes to seal the chicken.

5. Add the tomato puree, chicken stock, cream, bay leaf, cinnamon stick
   and salt to taste and bring to a simmer. Cook for 20 minutes or until the
   chicken is cooked through.

6. Scatter with coriander and serve with rice.

Did you
know?
While rice is an Indian staple, bread is also important. There are many different kinds of bread, such
as naan, roti, paratha and chapatti.

Pan-fried flat bread

This traditional Indian bread is called *paratha*. Serve warm from the pan with yoghurt raita or enjoy with a curry.

Makes 4 breads

Cooking and preparation time: 45 minutes

INGREDIENTS

FILLING

4 medium potatoes, peeled and cut into 2 cm cubes

3 tablespoons vegetable oil

1 tablespoon mustard seeds

1 tablespoon cumin seeds

2 long green chillies, finely chopped

5 cm piece of ginger, grated

1 cup peas

2 tablespoons garam marsala

1 tablespoon turmeric

sea salt and freshly ground black pepper

juice of ¹/₂ lemon

1 bunch coriander, chopped

DOUGH

3 cups atta flour

2 tablespoons vegetable oil

¹/₂ teaspoon sea salt

water

vegetable oil for frying
yoghurt or raita to serve

METHOD

1. Boil the potatoes in a saucepan of water until soft, then drain.

2. Heat the oil in a wok and add the mustard seeds, cumin seeds, chilli and ginger. Fry until the mixture is fragrant and the seeds start to pop, then add the potatoes, peas, garam marsala, turmeric and salt and pepper to taste. Stir for another minute, then remove from the heat. Stir in the lemon juice and coriander and leave to cool.

3. Combine the flour, oil and salt in a large bowl and add enough water to make a soft dough. Mix well with your hands. Leave the dough to rest for 5 minutes.

4. Take a quarter of the dough and shape into a ball. Place on a lightly floured work surface and roll out to a thin circle. Put a large dollop of filling in the centre, then bring in the edges of the circle to meet in the middle above the filling. Pinch the edges together to seal the filling inside and pull away any excess dough. Gently roll the dough out again to about 1 cm thick.

5. Heat a frying pan over medium heat. Add a little oil and place the bread in the pan. Cook for around 3 minutes on each side, until golden brown. While the bread is cooking, continue to roll out and fill the remaining breads and cook them one after the other with more oil as needed.

6. Serve warm with yoghurt or raita.

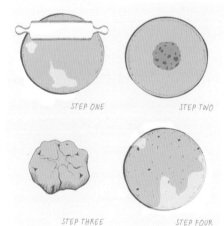

STEP ONE

STEP TWO

STEP THREE

STEP FOUR

RUSSIA

Russia experiences one of the longest and coldest winters in the world,

so delicious, warming soups and stews are important. Fresh fruit and vegetables are hard to grow, but cabbage is popular, and northern berries and mushrooms are abundant.

Chilled borscht

There are endless varieties of this soup found all over eastern and central Europe. They are generally based on beetroot, but can include many other vegetables. Some are served hot and some cold – this simple cold borscht is made lightly creamy with the addition of an egg.

Serves: 6

Cooking and preparation time: 1 hour and 45 minutes + refrigeration

INGREDIENTS

4 medium beetroots, peeled and cut into 4 wedges each
1.5 litres cold water
juice of 1 lemon
1 egg
1 tablespoon sugar
2 teaspoons sea salt
125 ml milk

TO SERVE

new potatoes, peeled, boiled and chilled
sour cream

METHOD

1. Put the beetroot and water in a saucepan and bring to the boil. Once boiling, turn the heat down to a simmer and cook without a lid (so the water reduces as the beetroot cooks) for around 1 hour, until the beetroot is tender. Around 15 minutes before the beetroot is cooked, add the lemon juice.

2. While the beetroot is cooking, combine the egg, salt and sugar in a large bowl and beat with a fork. Beat in the milk.

3. Scoop the hot beetroot from the cooking water and place in a blender or food processor. Also add a cup of the cooking water. Set the blender or food processor aside.

4. Pour the remaining hot cooking water into a heatproof jug. Slowly pour the hot water into the egg mixture, stirring constantly with the fork. The egg should lightly thicken the water and make it a little creamy.

5. Process the cooked beetroot and cup of cooking water until smooth. Stir into the egg mixture and leave the soup to cool. Once cool, chill in the refrigerator.

6. Serve the soup over chilled potatoes with dollops of sour cream.

beetroot water

egg mixture

Did you know?

Russian blini are small, thin pancakes made from either wheat or buckwheat. They symbolise the sun and are traditionally made at the end of winter during *Maslenitsa* (pancake week).

Beef stroganoff

Beef stroganoff is a delicious winter dish of beef and mushrooms laced with paprika and sour cream. It can be served with mashed potato, steamed rice or fettuccine.

Serves: 4

Cooking and preparation time: 1 hour and 40 minutes

INGREDIENTS

100 g (²/₃ cup) plain flour

2 tablespoons sweet paprika

1 teaspoon sea salt

500 g beef fillet, sliced into strips

3 tablespoons olive oil

40 g unsalted butter

300 g brown mushrooms, finely sliced

3 shallots, finely diced

2 tablespoons tomato paste

2 tablespoons worcestershire sauce

250 ml beef stock

250 ml sour cream

freshly ground black pepper

TO SERVE

500 g fettuccine

2 tablespoons extra-virgin olive oil

finely sliced spring onions or finely chopped flat-leaf parsley

METHOD

1. Before starting the stroganoff, bring a pot of salted water to boil for the fettucine. Once boiling, add the fettucine and stir to separate. Boil until just soft, then drain well, transfer to a large bowl and toss with the extra-virgin olive oil. Keep warm.

2. While the pasta is cooking, combine the flour, paprika and salt in a bowl. Add the sliced beef and toss well to coat.

3. Heat 2 tablespoons of the oil in a large frying pan over high heat. Add the beef and sear for 1–2 minutes, until browned all over. Transfer to a plate.

4. Reduce the heat of the pan to medium-high and add the remaining oil and half the butter. Add the mushrooms and sauté until soft.

5. Reduce the heat to medium, then add the remaining butter and the shallots. Sauté for a few more minutes.

Add sliced beef and sear until brown

6. Add the tomato paste, worcestershire sauce and stock and bring to the boil. Once boiling, reduce the heat to medium and stir in the sour cream and seared beef, plus any juices that have collected on the plate. When the beef has warmed through, turn off the heat and season to taste with salt and pepper.

7. Serve on top of the warm fettucine. Garnish with spring onions or parsley.

GREECE

Greece has a culinary history which
stretches back around 4000 years –
the very first recorded cookbook was written by
a Greek! Greek food has been influenced by Italy
and Turkey, and the cuisines of these Mediterranean
cultures share many characteristics.

Vegetable moussaka

Moussaka has similarities to lasagne, but instead of sheets of pasta it uses slices of eggplant – and in this case zucchini and potato. This is a vegetarian moussaka, but it can also be made with minced lamb.

Serves: 8-10

Cooking and preparation time: 95 minutes

INGREDIENTS

3 large eggplants, cut into 2 cm rounds

5 medium zucchini, cut lengthways into 1 cm slices

250 ml olive oil

2 large potatoes, peeled and cut into 1 cm slices

1 cup fresh breadcrumbs

1 cup grated cheddar cheese

TOMATO SAUCE

2 tablespoons olive oil

1 large onion, finely chopped

2 garlic cloves, finely chopped

800 g tin diced tomatoes

2 tablespoons tomato paste

1 tablespoon dried oregano

1 teaspoon ground cinnamon

sea salt and freshly ground black pepper

BÉCHAMEL SAUCE

500 ml milk

50 g unsalted butter

2 tablespoons plain flour

1 teaspoon sea salt

2 eggs, beaten

½ cup freshly grated parmesan

METHOD

1. To make the tomato sauce, heat the oil in a heavy-based saucepan over medium heat. Add the onion and cook until soft. Add the garlic, stirring well, then add the remaining ingredients, seasoning to taste with salt and pepper. Cover with a lid, bring to a simmer, and cook for around 30 minutes, stirring occasionally. Then, remove the lid and simmer for another 30 minutes.

2. While the tomato sauce is cooking, prepare the béchamel sauce. Pour the milk into a small saucepan and heat gently. Meanwhile, melt the butter in a heavy-based saucepan over medium heat. Whisk the flour into the butter and cook, continuing to whisk, for 2-3 minutes. Whisk in the salt and remove from the heat.

3. Slowly pour the hot milk into the flour mixture, whisking until combined. Return the saucepan to the heat and cook until thick, whisking constantly. Remove from heat.

4. Slowly pour the beaten egg into the sauce, whisking until combined, then whisk in the parmesan. Set aside.

5. Heat a barbecue grill or a frying pan to very hot. Lightly brush some eggplant slices with a little of the oil and grill for 2 minutes on each side. Continue grilling the remaining eggplant slices and then the zucchini slices.

6. Heat the remaining oil in a frying pan and gently fry the potato slices for around 5 minutes on each side, until golden. Drain on paper towel.

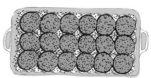

eggplant slices + cheese and breadcrumbs

7. Preheat the oven to 180°C. Arrange a layer of potatoes in the base of a large baking dish. Add a layer of grilled eggplant. Sprinkle with breadcrumbs and cheese. Add a layer of grilled zucchini and cover with tomato sauce. Repeat the layers of potato, eggplant, zucchini and tomato sauce.

zucchini slices

8. Cover the moussaka with the béchamel sauce and sprinkle with the remaining breadcrumbs and cheese. Bake in the oven for around 45 minutes, or until golden brown.

red sauce

Loukoumades

Loukoumades are small donuts served with sugar syrup or honey.
They make a great snack or dessert.

Makes about 30 loukoumades

Cooking and preparation time: 2 hours

INGREDIENTS

440 ml milk

100 g unsalted butter at room
temperature, diced

75 g (¹/₃ cup) caster sugar

4 eggs

20 g fresh yeast
(or 2¹/₄ teaspoons dried yeast)

600 g (4 cups) plain flour

¹/₂ teaspoon sea salt

vegetable oil for deep-frying

2 teaspoons ground cinnamon

185 ml honey

METHOD

1. Pour the milk into a saucepan and heat until warm. Whisk in the butter, sugar and eggs until the butter has melted and the mixture is well combined.

2. Put the fresh yeast in a small bowl and break it up with your fingers until smooth. If using dried yeast, you can skip this. Add about half cup of the warm milk mixture and mix well. Leave for 5 minutes, then stir in the remaining milk mixture.

3. Combine the flour and salt in a large bowl and make a well in the centre. Slowly pour in the milk mixture, whisking until smooth. Cover with plastic wrap and set aside to prove in a warm place for 45 minutes–1 hour, or until roughly tripled in size.

4. Pour vegetable oil into a large saucepan until one-third full and place over medium heat. Heat to 165°C (test the temperature by dropping in a small cube of bread – it should start frying not too vigorously).

5. Take a tablespoon of dough from the bowl and use a second spoon to scoop the dough off the spoon into the hot oil (aiming to create a fairly neat ball). Continue scooping dough into the oil until you have filled the oil with a layer of loukoumades. Fry for 3–4 minutes, until golden and cooked through. Drain on paper towel. Cook loukoumades in batches until you have used all the dough.

6. Dust the hot loukoumades with cinnamon and drizzle with honey.

Did you know?

Meze – tasty bites such as olives, dolmades (stuffed vine leaves), saganaki (fried or grilled cheese), or a selection of dips – are a popular way for people to share food in a social gathering in Greece.

ITALY

Italian cooking evolved from rustic home cooking; to this day, it is one of the simplest and most popular cuisines in the world. Some traditional Italian recipes require only a few ingredients – the quality and freshness of ingredients is much more important than the complexity of recipes.

Pumpkin and ricotta gnocchi

Gnocchi are handmade pasta dumplings. They are usually made from potato, but can also be made with pumpkin. You can add extra herbs such as sage to the sauce, and don't forget the parmesan on top.

Serves: 6

Cooking and preparation time: 60 minutes

INGREDIENTS

GNOCCHI

500 g pumpkin, skinned, seeded and cut into 2 cm cubes

olive oil

750 g fresh ricotta

2 egg yolks

200 g (1 1/3 cups) plain flour

pinch of ground nutmeg

sea salt and freshly ground black pepper

SAUCE AND GARNISH

6 slices of prosciutto

1 tablespoon unsalted butter

1 tablespoon olive oil

1 small red onion, sliced

2 garlic cloves, finely chopped

5 flat-leaf parsley stalks

700 ml cream

100 g baby red chard or spinach

1/2 cup freshly grated parmesan

1/2 teaspoon sea salt

1/2 teaspoon freshly ground black pepper

2 tablespoons chopped flat-leaf parsley

METHOD

1. Preheat the oven to 200°C. Put the pumpkin on an oven tray and toss with a small drizzle of olive oil. Roast for 15–20 minutes, or until soft and golden.

2. Tip the hot pumpkin into a large bowl and add the ricotta, egg yolks, flour, nutmeg, and salt and pepper to taste. Mix with your hands, breaking up the pumpkin and ricotta until the mixture is smooth.

3. Bring a pot of water to boil. Scoop the gnocchi mixture into a large piping bag without a nozzle. When the water is boiling, hold the bag over the water and pipe a dumpling about 2.5 cm wide into the water, using a skewer to cut it from the tip of the bag. Continue piping gnocchi into the water until you have used about a third of the mixture.

Cut the dumplings from the tip of the piping bag

4. Scoop the gnocchi out of the water when they float to the surface, and place in a colander. Continue cooking the rest of the gnocchi in another 2 batches. Spread the cooked gnocchi out over a lightly oiled oven tray.

5. Reheat the oven to 180°C. Line a small oven tray with baking paper and lay the prosciutto slices on top. Bake for around 5 minutes, until crisp.

6. Melt the butter and oil in a large saucepan over medium heat. Add the onion, garlic and parsley stalks and sauté for about 4 minutes, until softened but not browned. Add the cream and simmer until lightly reduced.

7. While the sauce is simmering, put the tray of gnocchi into the oven for around 4 minutes, until heated through.

8. Pick out the parsley stalks from the sauce and add the chard or spinach, half the parmesan, and the salt and pepper. Simmer for another 3–4 minutes.

9. Serve the gnocchi topped with the sauce. Sprinkle with the remaining parmesan and the parsley, and garnish with the crispy prosciutto.

Tiramisu

This version of Italy's classic dessert is served in glasses, although it can also be made in a large bowl or dish and cut or scooped into portions. For an extra chocolate hit, add grated chocolate between the layers.

Serves: 8

Cooking and preparation time: 45 minutes

INGREDIENTS

175 g (1 ¹/₃ cups) icing sugar

1 ¹/₂ tablespoons Dutch cocoa, plus extra to dust

90 ml hot water

150 ml espresso coffee

3 egg yolks

300 ml cream

250 g mascarpone

1 teaspoon vanilla extract

32 sponge fingers (savoiardi)

METHOD

1. Combine 130 g (1 cup) of the icing sugar and the cocoa in a large bowl and slowly whisk in the hot water, mixing to a smooth, runny sauce. Whisk in the coffee and leave the mixture to cool to room temperature.

2. Put the egg yolks and remaining icing sugar in a separate bowl and beat with electric beaters for around 5 minutes, until pale, thick and increased in volume. When you lift the beaters out, they should leave a ribbon-like trail of egg mixture that should hold its shape for a while.

3. Whip the cream to soft peaks in a separate bowl. Add the mascarpone and vanilla and beat briefly until just combined. Use a spatula to gently fold the mascarpone cream into the egg mixture.

4. Roughly crumble the sponge fingers into pieces of about 1 cm into the bowl of coffee and chocolate sauce. Stir so the pieces become evenly soaked.

5. Divide half the soaked sponge pieces between 8 serving glasses. Spoon half the cream mixture on top.

6. Top with the remaining sponge pieces, followed by the remaining cream mixture. Refrigerate overnight.

7. To serve, remove the tiramisu glasses from the refrigerator and dust with cocoa.

Sponge fingers

Did you know? Pasta is a staple of Italian cooking, and may be dry or fresh. It comes in an amazing variety of shapes, sizes and colours: spaghetti, macaroni and lasagne are just a few pastas popular around the world.

FRANCE

is a nation of food lovers.

French lunchtimes can be up to two hours long
– even on weekdays! Cheese features in many
French recipes; in fact, France produces over
300 different types of cheeses, including Gruyère,
and the famously smelly Epoisses cheese.

Soufflé chou-fleur

'*Chou-fleur*' means cauliflower in French. This classic savoury soufflé features cauliflower and several types of cheese, including cream cheese, parmesan and Gruyère.

Serves: 8

Cooking and preparation time: 90 minutes

INGREDIENTS

1 medium cauliflower, separated into florets

2 tablespoons lemon juice

unsalted butter to coat the ramekins

finely grated parmesan to coat the ramekins

125 g cream cheese at room temperature

5 eggs, separated

3 tablespoons crème fraîche

3 tablespoons freshly grated parmesan

2 tablespoons grated gruyère

1 bunch chives, finely chopped

1/4 teaspoon sea salt

1/4 teaspoon freshly ground white pepper

1/4 teaspoon ground nutmeg

METHOD

1. Put the cauliflower in a large bowl and dress with the lemon juice. Transfer to a steamer and steam for 4–5 minutes, or until tender. Return the cauliflower to the bowl and leave to cool slightly, then puree with a stick blender. Scrape into a smaller bowl.

2. Preheat the oven to 190°C. Butter 8 individual ramekins and sprinkle the insides with a layer of finely grated parmesan for a cheesy coating.

3. Put the cream cheese in the large bowl used for the cauliflower and beat with electric beaters until smooth and creamy. Add the egg yolks one at a time, beating well after each addition. Stir in the cauliflower, crème fraîche, grated cheeses, chives, salt, pepper and nutmeg.

4. Put the egg whites in a large clean bowl and beat with clean beaters until soft peaks form. Use a spatula to gently fold the egg whites into the cauliflower mixture, just until you can no longer see streaks of egg white.

5. Spoon the mixture into the prepared ramekins, filling to the top. Smooth the tops with the spatula, then run the tip of your thumb around the rim of the soufflés to create a shallow channel to help with rising. Place the soufflés on an oven tray.

6. Bake in the oven for 25 minutes, or until risen and golden on top. Make sure you don't open the door to check progress until you're certain the soufflés are done, as a draft of air can deflate them. Serve straight from the oven.

Cauliflower

France is divided into regions, each with its own cooking style, produce and flavours. Some famous French products are even named after the places they originated, such as Dijon mustard from Dijon, and Quiche Lorraine from the Lorraine region.

Crêpes with strawberries

Crêpes are eaten for breakfast, lunch, dinner or dessert in France. Fillings can be either savoury or sweet, from cheese and ham to chocolate sauce. These sweet crêpes are served with a simple mix of strawberries tossed with sugar and lemon juice.

Serves: 4

Cooking and preparation time: 60 minutes

INGREDIENTS

CRÊPES

1 cup (150 g) plain flour
1 1/2 tablespoons caster sugar
pinch of sea salt
2 eggs
375 ml milk
40 g unsalted butter, melted, plus extra butter for frying

STRAWBERRIES

1 punnet of strawberries, hulled and quartered
3 tablespoons icing sugar
juice of 1/2 lemon

METHOD

1. Sieve the flour, sugar and salt into a bowl. Make a well in the centre and crack in the eggs, then pour in the milk. Whisk to a smooth batter. Add the melted butter and whisk again. Strain into another bowl to remove any lumps and refrigerate for 30 minutes.

2. Combine the strawberries, icing sugar and lemon juice in a bowl and set aside.

3. Heat a frying pan over medium-high heat. Add a little butter and spread it across the pan, then add a ladleful of crêpe batter. Tilt the pan to spread the batter out to a thin crêpe. Cook for 1–2 minutes until golden, then flip and cook the other side for a minute. Transfer to a plate and continue cooking crêpes with the remaining batter. Separate each newly cooked crêpe with a sheet of baking paper to prevent the crêpes from sticking to each other.

4. To serve, fold the warm crêpes into quarters and top with the strawberries.

UNITED KINGDOM

English cooking was traditionally quite simple.

Medieval meals included bread and cheese, roasted meats,
fish, stews, soups, vegetables and puddings.
Today, English cuisine includes many
dishes influenced by India, China
and European countries.

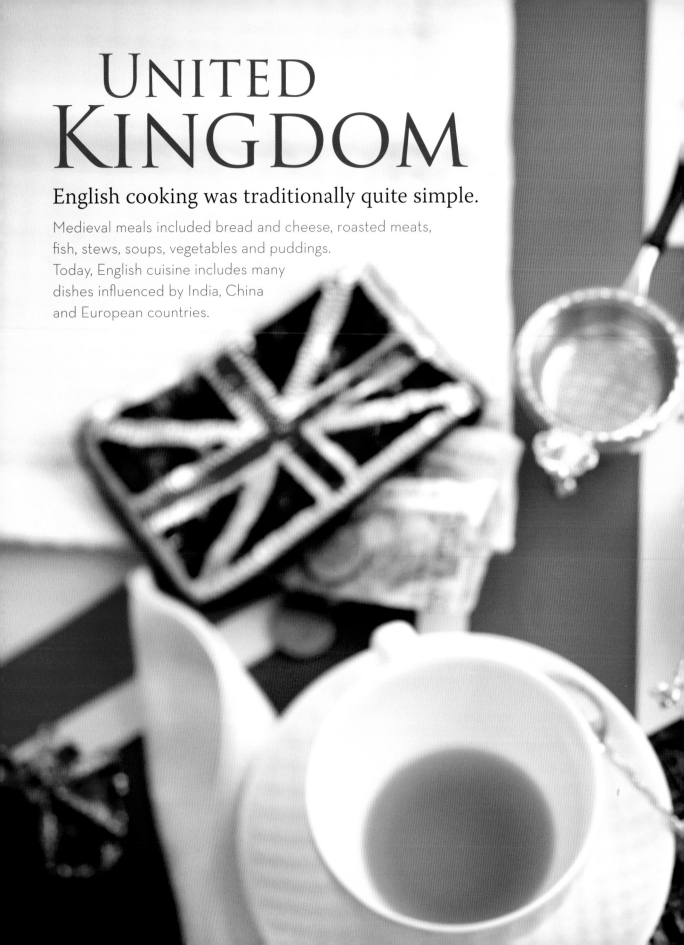

Beef rib roast with horseradish mascarpone

A beef rib roast is the perfect dinner if you want to impress! Serve it with roast potatoes and pumpkin, and don't forget a green vegetable. For the full English experience, you might also like to serve it with Yorkshire puddings. Yorkshire puddings are perfect for mopping up gravy, juices or sauce.

Serves: 8

Cooking and preparation time: 2 hours + 4 hours for yorkshire puddings

INGREDIENTS

5 kg beef standing rib roast, frenched (ask your butcher to do this for you)

100 ml olive oil

6 garlic cloves, crushed

small handful of rosemary leaves, chopped

3 teaspoons sea salt

1 teaspoon freshly ground black pepper

HORSERADISH MASCARPONE

100 ml cream

300 g mascarpone

4 cm piece of fresh horseradish, peeled and grated (or 3 tablespoons from a jar)

1/2 bunch flat-leaf parsley, finely chopped

YORKSHIRE PUDDINGS

250 g (1 2/3 cups) plain flour

2 eggs

250 ml milk

250 ml water

150 ml olive oil, plus extra for the trays

pinch of sea salt

METHOD

1. Preheat the oven to 220°C. Combine the oil, garlic, rosemary, salt and pepper in a small bowl. Place the beef on an oven tray and brush the mixture over the top. Rub the mixture into the beef with your fingers, coating well.

2. Roast the beef in the oven for 15 minutes, then reduce the temperature to 180°C and roast for another 1 1/4 hours.

3. While the beef is cooking, make the horseradish mascarpone. Whip the cream, then mix in the mascarpone, horseradish and parsley.

4. When the beef is cooked, allow it to rest at room temperature uncovered for 20–30 minutes. Then carve between each rib and serve with the horseradish mascarpone.

BRUSH OIL MIXTURE

YORKSHIRE PUDDINGS

1. Combine the ingredients in a food processor and process for 2–3 minutes. Then leave the batter to rest for at least 3 hours.

2. Preheat the oven to 200°C. Using a muffin tray, put 1 tablespoon of oil into each of 10 large muffin holes and heat in the oven for 5 minutes, or until very hot.

3. Pulse the batter in the food processor again, then pour into the hot muffin holes. Bake for 25 minutes, or until risen and golden.

4. Turn the tray upside down and tap the puddings out. Serve hot with roast beef.

Nana's apple pie

This apple pie doesn't have a pastry lid, and the pastry is simply squashed into the tin rather than being rolled out with a rolling pin, so it's a fun and easy pie to make. And don't forget the whipped cream or ice-cream!

Serves: 6

Cooking and preparation time: 70 minutes

INGREDIENTS

PASTRY

125 g unsalted butter at room temperature, diced

165 g (³/4 cup) caster sugar

1 egg

150 g (1 cup) plain flour

75 g (¹/2 cup) self-raising flour

APPLES

800 g tin sliced apples or 1.5 kg fresh apples, peeled and cored.

1 teaspoon ground cinnamon

1 teaspoon ground nutmeg

3 tablespoons white sugar

METHOD

1. Put the butter and sugar in a mixing bowl and beat with electric beaters until pale and creamy. Beat in the egg.

2. Stir in the flours. Transfer the dough to a lightly floured work surface and knead briefly.

3. Preheat the oven to 180°C and lightly butter a 25 cm pie dish.

4. Take a ball of dough and form it into a sausage. Stick it around a section of the rim of the dish, flattening it to about 2 cm thick. Take another ball of dough and repeat. Keep doing this until you have a thick rim of pastry all the way around the dish.

5. Keep flattening balls of dough over the base of the dish, more thinly now. Squash each piece of dough together so there are no gaps in the pastry.

6. Combine the apples, spices and sugar in a bowl. Spoon into the pastry base. Bake in the oven for 40 minutes, or until the pastry is golden.

Pastry

A popular English tradition is the Sunday roast. This dish developed because there was time on Sunday for the slow cooking needed for the meat. It also showed your neighbours that you could afford a special meal.

Spain

is almost completely surrounded by water,

so typical Spanish menus are crammed with fresh seafood dishes. Ham (*jamón*) is widely eaten in Spain, and pork from the black Iberian pig is considered a specialty.

Gazpacho

Gazpacho is a vibrant summer tomato soup that is served chilled. This version has a garnish of finely diced capsicum, cucumber and croutons, but you can also serve it topped with chives or chopped boiled egg.

Serves: 4-6

Cooking and preparation time: 90 minutes

INGREDIENTS

1 kg ripe tomatoes, chopped

1 medium red capsicum, chopped

1 red onion, chopped

1 garlic clove, finely chopped

400 ml water

2 1/2 tablespoons extra-virgin olive oil

1 tablespoon white wine vinegar

1 teaspoon pepper

1 tablespoon sugar

1 teaspoon sea salt

TO GARNISH

finely diced red capsicum

finely diced cucumber

bread cut into small cubes and fried to make croutons

METHOD

1. Mix all the ingredients in a large bowl and leave to marinate for 1 hour.

2. Transfer to a blender or food processor and puree for 2 minutes on high speed. If there is too much mixture to fit in the machine in one go, do this in a few batches.

3. Strain the liquid through a fine sieve back into the bowl.

4. Taste for seasoning, add if needed, and chill in the refrigerator.

5. Serve the cold soup garnished with diced red capsicum, cucumber and croutons.

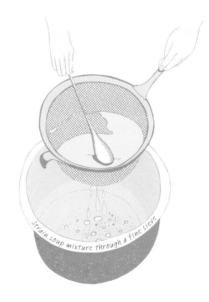

Strain soup mixture through a fine sieve

Did you know?

Spanish people love tasty snacks called pinchos, or tapas. There are many tapas bars in Spain where people gather before lunch or dinner for a pre-meal snack.

Paella

Paella is a dish of rice, meat, seafood and vegetables cooked in a wide and shallow pan.
It has many variations — this one includes chicken, chorizo, mussels and prawns.

Serves: 8

**Cooking and preparation
time:** 80 minutes

INGREDIENTS

2 tablespoons olive oil

1 onion, finely chopped

2 garlic cloves, finely chopped

200 g chicken thigh fillet, diced

2 chorizo sausages, sliced

2 tablespoons sherry vinegar

1 teaspoon saffron threads

3 teaspoons smoked paprika

sea salt and freshly ground black
pepper

500 ml tomato puree

2 litres chicken stock

500 g paella rice such as calasparra

8 shelled raw prawns

500 g mussels, cleaned and de-bearded

300 g peas

2 tablespoons chopped flat-leaf
parsley

2 lemons, cut into wedges

METHOD

1. Heat the oil in a large paella pan or frying pan over medium-high heat. Add the onion and garlic and fry until the onion is soft. Add the chicken and chorizo and fry until the chicken is golden and cooked through. Spoon the chicken and sausage onto a plate, leaving most of the onion, garlic and oil behind.

2. Return the pan to the heat and add the sherry vinegar to deglaze the pan.

3. Add the saffron, paprika, salt and pepper and cook briefly, stirring, until aromatic.

4. Stir in the tomato puree and cook for 20 minutes, or until lightly reduced.

5. While the tomato is cooking, pour the stock into a saucepan and heat to simmering.

6. Stir the rice and half the hot stock into the tomato sauce and bring to a gentle simmer. Cook for 15 minutes without stirring. Pour in more stock if the rice starts looking dry.

7. Push the prawns and mussels into the surface of the paella and scatter with the peas. Cover the paella with foil and continue to cook gently for another 10 minutes, or until the rice is tender, the prawns are cooked and the mussels have opened. Keep checking underneath the foil and adding more stock as needed - but allow the rice to absorb the stock at the end.

8. Remove the foil and scatter the chicken and chorizo over the paella, using the spoon to lightly bury the meat in the rice. Remove the pan from the heat.

9. Leave the paella to stand for 10 minutes, then garnish with parsley and serve with lemon wedges.

Morocco

Moroccan cuisine is famous for its rich, earthy flavours.

Spices made from dried seeds, roots, and barks are used extensively, giving Moroccan food its amazing colour and taste. Common spices include turmeric, ginger, cumin, chilli powder, and *ras el hanout* (a spice blend).

Lamb, date and cinnamon tagine

While this tagine is made with diced lamb, it can also be made with lamb shanks for an elegant and impressive meal. Tagines are commonly flavoured with preserved lemon, but here a scored fresh lemon is used for a similar flavour. Serve with couscous.

Serves: 4

Cooking and preparation time: 2 hours

INGREDIENTS

1 small lemon

75 g unsalted butter

700 g diced lamb from a shoulder or leg

2 onions, roughly chopped

3 garlic cloves, finely chopped

1/2 teaspoon cumin seeds, ground

1/2 teaspoon coriander seeds, ground

1 teaspoon ground cinnamon

1 teaspoon ground ginger

1/2 teaspoon cayenne pepper

500 ml veal or beef stock

3 carrots, cut into large dice

1 cinnamon stick

2 tablespoons honey

1 large bunch coriander, chopped

sea salt and freshly ground black pepper

400 g tin chickpeas, drained

12 pitted dates

1/2 teaspoon saffron threads

METHOD

1. Hold the lemon in one hand and with a small, sharp knife in the other hand, carefully cut lots of small crosses all over the lemon skin. This will help release the flavour.

2. Melt the butter in a heavy-based pot and add the lamb, onion, garlic and ground spices. Cook, stirring, for about 3 minutes, allowing the meat to become lightly seared and well coated in the butter and spices.

3. Pour on the stock and add the scored lemon, carrot, cinnamon stick, honey and half the coriander. Season with some salt and pepper and bring to a simmer. Cover with a lid and cook very gently for about 1 1/2 hours, or until the lamb is tender.

4. Remove the lemon and discard. Add the chickpeas, dates and saffron to the pot and simmer uncovered until the sauce is fairly thick.

5. Taste and adjust the seasoning. Serve the tagine on couscous scattered with the remaining coriander.

melt butter

Did you know?

Couscous is a popular side dish in Northern Africa. It is eaten in place of rice or bread. It is made from coarsely-ground semolina (large, hard grains of wheat).

Baklava with labneh and pomegranate molasses

Baklava is a sweet layered pastry filled with ground nuts. In this recipe it is made into an impressive dessert with a scoop of yoghurt (labneh) and a drizzle of pomegranate molasses. Begin this recipe the day before by draining the yoghurt overnight.

Makes 8 serves with labneh and pomegranate molasses, plus extra baklava

Cooking and preparation time: 1 hour and 45 minutes + overnight

INGREDIENTS

LABNEH

250 ml Greek yoghurt

pinch of sea salt

BAKLAVA

150 g walnuts

150 g pistachios

3 tablespoons white sugar

2 teaspoons ground cinnamon

375 g packet of filo pastry

180 g unsalted butter, melted

2 teaspoons water

HONEY SYRUP

500 g honey

165 g (³/4 cup) white sugar

250 ml water

1 lemon, zested and juiced

3 tablespoons orange-blossom water

pomegranate molasses to serve

METHOD

1. Prepare the labneh by mixing the yoghurt and salt in a bowl. Scoop into a square of muslin and tie the corners. Put the bundle in a sieve set over a bowl and leave in the refrigerator to let the whey drain off overnight.

2. The next day, preheat the oven to 180°C. To make the filling, spread the walnuts on a tray and lightly roast for 5–8 minutes. Leave to cool.

3. Combine the walnuts, pistachios, sugar and cinnamon in a food processor and process until the nuts are finely chopped.

4. Unroll the filo pastry onto a work surface. Cut all the sheets in half. When you're not using the filo, cover it with a dry tea towel followed by a damp tea towel to keep it from drying out.

5. Brush a shallow 20 x 30 cm tin with some melted butter. Remove a third of the filo sheets from the stack. Brush one sheet with butter, then lay the sheet in the base of the tin. Brush the top of the sheet with butter. Repeat with the remaining third of filo.

6. Scatter a third of the nut mixture over the top of the filo. Then repeat the process with the next third of filo, buttering and layering the sheets. Scatter another third of nuts over the top. Continue layering the final third of filo, scattering the nuts over the top before layering on a few final sheets of filo. Make sure you brush the very top sheet with butter.

7. Reheat the oven to 180°C. Use a sharp knife to cut a diamond pattern (with the diamonds measuring about 5 cm) in the top layer of filo. Sprinkle the top of the baklava with the water. Bake in the oven for 30 minutes, then cover with foil and cook for another 45 minutes.

8. While the baklava is baking, put the ingredients for the honey syrup other than the orange-blossom water in a saucepan and bring to the boil. Cook until syrupy, then remove from heat and add the orange-blossom water. Leave to cool.

9. Remove the baklava from the oven. Pour the syrup evenly over the hot baklava. Leave the baklava to cool completely.

10. Re-cut the diamonds in the baklava, this time going all the way to the base. Serve with small dollops of labneh and a drizzle of pomegranate molasses.

UNITED STATES OF
AMERICA

Modern American cuisine is a fusion of the foods of many cultures from around the world who have settled in the United States, as well as the traditional foods of Native Americans. Regional foods include clam chowder from New England, Molokai shrimp from Hawaii, and fried green tomatoes, which are popular in the South.

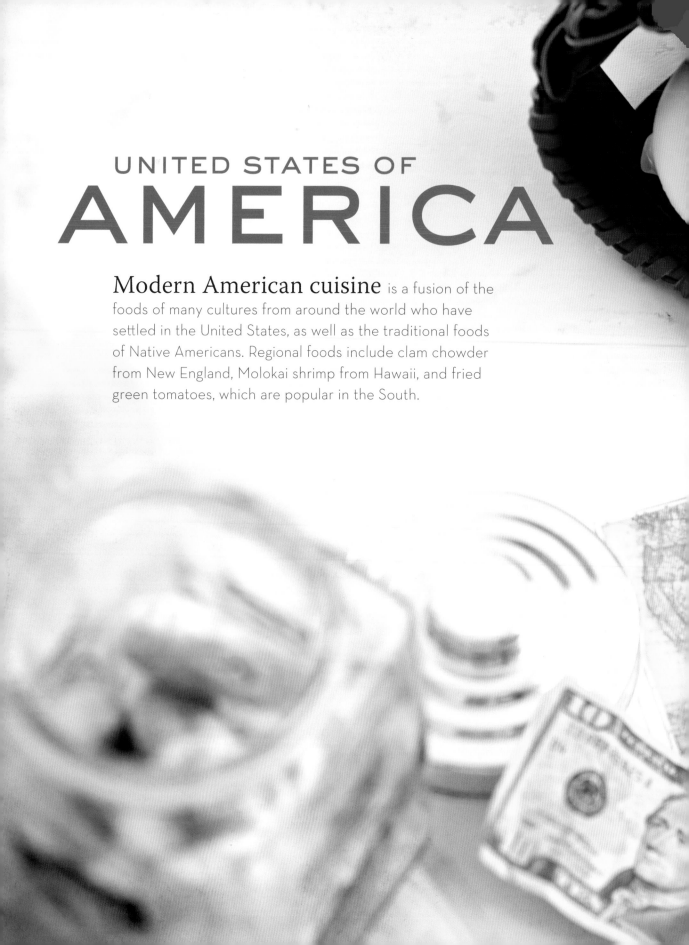

Beef burgers

Just about everyone enjoys a burger, especially one with all the trimmings! Choose your favourite fillings and condiments – you can even swap the minced beef for chicken.

Serves: 4

Cooking and preparation time: 30 minutes

INGREDIENTS

500 g minced beef
1/2 onion, finely chopped
2 garlic cloves, crushed
1/2 cup fresh breadcrumbs
3 tablespoons chopped flat-leaf parsley
3 tablespoons chopped thyme
1 egg
1 teaspoon sea salt
1 teaspoon freshly ground black pepper
1 1/2 tablespoons olive oil
4 hamburger buns

OPTIONAL FILLINGS

onions, sliced
smoked bacon
eggs
slices of cheddar cheese
gherkins, sliced
tomato, sliced
lettuce leaves
tomato chutney
dijon mustard
mayonnaise or aioli

METHOD

1. Combine the beef, onion, garlic, breadcrumbs, herbs, egg and salt and pepper in a mixing bowl. Mix well with your hands then shape into 4 large patties.

2. Heat the oil in a frying pan and fry the burgers on both sides until browned and cooked through. Alternatively, cook the burgers on a barbecue.

3. Keep the burgers warm on a tray in a low oven as you fry onions, bacon or eggs as desired or while you prepare other fillings. Warm the buns in the oven or toast them in a toaster.

4. To serve, put the burgers inside the buns with your favourite combination of fillings and condiments.

shape beef burger

Immigrant influences on food in America include Tex-Mex (Texan/Mexican fusion), such as chilli con carne and nachos. Creole and Cajun cooking, popular in the southern American states, reflect the influence of French and Spanish settlers.

The world's best chocolate brownie

A chocolate brownie is the perfect lunch box treat – or a delicious dessert if you add strawberries and cream. This one has pecans and is beautifully fudgy from the long, slow cooking time.

Serves: 15

Cooking and preparation time: 60 minutes

INGREDIENTS

370 g unsalted butter

520 g dark chocolate, broken into pieces

7 eggs

540 g (2 ½ cups) caster sugar

90 g (¾ cup) gluten-free flour

90 g (¾ cup) Dutch cocoa

2 teaspoons baking powder

225 g pecans, chopped

METHOD

1. Preheat the oven to 150°C. Butter a 25 x 36 cm cake tin and line the base and sides with baking paper.

2. Put the butter and chocolate in a bowl over a saucepan and place over low heat. Stir until melted and smooth, then remove from the heat.

3. Put the eggs and sugar in a large bowl and beat with electric beaters for around 5 minutes, until pale, thick and increased in volume. When you lift the beaters out, they should leave a ribbon-like trail of egg mixture that should hold its shape for a while.

4. Sift the flour, baking powder and cocoa into another large bowl. Stir in the pecans. Add the chocolate and egg mixtures and use a spatula to fold together until well combined.

5. Scrape the mixture into the tin and bake in the oven for 40 minutes, or until just set. Let the brownie cool completely in the tin.

6. Remove the brownie from the tin and cut into squares or fingers. Serve with icy cold milk.

MEXICO

Beans, rice, and corn are
staple foods in Mexico;
corn *(maize)* is thought to have first been
cultivated in prehistoric times by the people
of southern Mexico. Several species of
chilli are native to Mexico, and chilli is an
important ingredient in Mexican cooking.

Chicken fajitas

Fajitas – pronounced 'fa-heetas' – can be made with chicken, lamb, beef or pork, and are a fun, colourful and tasty meal at any time of day. This recipe includes sweet sautéed capsicum, but you can keep the capsicum raw and crunchy if you prefer.

Serves: 8

Cooking and preparation time: 90 minutes

INGREDIENTS

1 kg chicken thigh fillets, cut into 2 cm slices
2 garlic cloves, crushed
2 teaspoons smoked paprika
1/2 teaspoon ground cumin
100 ml olive oil
1 green capsicum, sliced
1 red capsicum, sliced
1 yellow capsicum, sliced
8 tortillas
grated tasty cheese to serve
1 iceberg lettuce, shredded, to serve
crème fraîche, sour cream or natural yoghurt to serve

TOMATO AND AVOCADO SALSA

5 medium-sized ripe tomatoes, chopped
2 avocados, chopped
1 red onion, finely chopped
1 garlic clove, crushed
1 small red chilli, finely chopped
1/2 cup finely chopped coriander
1 teaspoon finely grated lemon zest
1 tablespoon lemon juice
2 tablespoons extra-virgin olive oil
sea salt and freshly ground black pepper
sugar

METHOD

1. Put the chicken strips in a bowl and add the garlic, spices and 3 tablespoons of the oil. Mix well and leave to marinate for 40 minutes.

2. Heat the remaining oil in a frying pan and add the sliced capsicums. Gently sauté until soft.

3. Combine the ingredients for the salsa, adding salt, pepper and a little sugar to taste.

4. Preheat a barbecue grill or grill pan over high heat. Cook the marinated chicken strips for around 5 minutes, turning occasionally, until browned and cooked through. Transfer to a tray and cover with foil to keep warm.

5. Warm the tortillas on the grill until lightly charred.

6. To serve, top a tortilla with chicken, capsicum and salsa. Add cheese, lettuce and a dollop of sour cream or yoghurt. Wrap the tortilla around the filling and enjoy.

Chocolate is an important part of Mexican history; cacao (cocoa) seeds were first made into drinks by the indigenous Mayan and the Aztec peoples. Cocoa powder is used in savoury dishes such as mole sauce, as well as in sweet foods.

Grilled bananas with chilli and mint chocolate sauce

This sauce is delicious with grilled bananas, but is also great over ice-cream and strawberries. For an authentic Mexican touch, use Ibarra chocolate, which is flavoured with cinnamon. Alternatively you can use dark chocolate. Leave out the chilli if you prefer, or add more if you like it hot!

Serves: 4

Cooking and preparation time: 40 minutes

INGREDIENTS

50 g unsalted butter

3 tablespoons brown sugar

4 firm-ripe bananas, peeled and cut in half lengthwise

SAUCE

250 ml cream

1/2 bunch mint

1 long red chilli, seeded and finely sliced

150 g Ibarra or dark chocolate, broken into pieces

120 ml sweet chilli sauce

METHOD

1. Put the cream, mint sprigs and sliced chilli in a saucepan and place over gentle heat. Remove from the heat just before the cream boils and leave to infuse for about 1 hour.

2. Strain the cream into a bowl and add the chocolate. Set the bowl over a saucepan of boiling water and whisk until the chocolate is melted and the mixture is smooth.

3. Whisk in the sweet chilli sauce and set aside.

4. Melt the butter in an ovenproof frying pan and stir in the brown sugar. Add the bananas and gently toss in the butter and sugar.

5. Place the pan underneath a grill and cook until the bananas are golden.

6. Serve the bananas with the chocolate sauce spooned over the top.

Cut the bananas in half

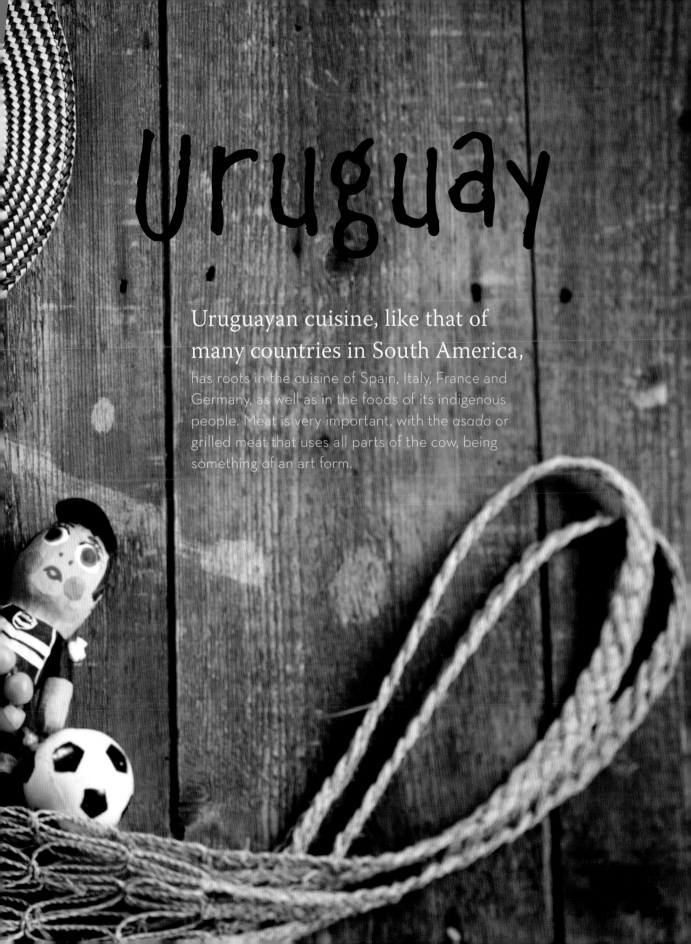

Uruguay

**Uruguayan cuisine, like that of
many countries in South America,**
has roots in the cuisine of Spain, Italy, France and
Germany, as well as in the foods of its indigenous
people. Meat is very important, with the *asado* or
grilled meat that uses all parts of the cow, being
something of an art form.

Albóndigas

These mouth-watering chicken or turkey meatballs can be served with bread, pasta or rice. Change the meat to lamb or beef if you prefer, or serve with a side of crusty bread.

Serves: 4

Cooking and preparation time: 60 minutes

INGREDIENTS

2 medium onions, quartered

2 garlic cloves

400 g minced chicken or turkey

100 g bacon, finely chopped

1/2 cup fresh breadcrumbs

1 1/2 tablespoons soy sauce

1 teaspoon dried oregano

plain flour

olive oil

1 tablespoon chopped flat-leaf parsley

4 ripe tomatoes, chopped

1 medium carrot, grated

125 ml chicken stock

2 tablespoons tomato paste

2 cloves

1 bay leaf

sea salt and freshly ground black pepper

1 cup peas

METHOD

1. Put the onion and garlic in a food processor and blend to a purée.

2. Tip half into a large bowl and add the chicken, bacon, breadcrumbs, soy sauce and oregano. Mix well with your hands.

3. Form the mixture into small balls about the size of large marbles. Roll the balls lightly in flour as you go, and set aside on a plate.

4. Heat a little oil in a large saucepan and add the remaining onion and garlic, and the parsley. Cook gently until soft, then stir in the tomato, carrot, stock, tomato paste, cloves, bay leaf, and some salt and pepper to taste. Simmer for 5 minutes, then remove from the heat.

5. Heat a thin layer of oil in a frying pan. Add enough meatballs to fill the pan and fry gently until browned all over. When the meatballs are cooked, drop them into the sauce, and continue frying the rest of the meatballs.

6. Once all the meatballs have been added to the sauce, simmer for about 30 minutes. Stir in the peas to cook for the last 3 minutes.

Make small balls with the meat mixture.

Did you know? Dulce de leche is a caramel spread that is widely popular in South America. It is used in many Uruguayan desserts, and is also eaten with cookies, crêpes, bread and pastries.

Alfajores

Alfajores are shortbread-style biscuits sandwiched with a wicked filling of dulce de leche – a milk caramel adored by South Americans from Peru to Argentina. It requires lengthy cooking, but is worth the effort!

Makes about 24 biscuits

Cooking and preparation time: 60 minutes + 2–3 hours for dulce de leche

INGREDIENTS

DULCE DE LECHE

1 litre milk

440 g (2 cups) white sugar

1 teaspoon bicarbonate of soda

1 tablespoon vanilla extract

BISCUITS

130 g (1 cup) cornflour

260 g (1 3/4 cups) plain flour

1/2 teaspoon baking powder

1/2 teaspoon sea salt

250 g unsalted butter, diced

110 g (1/2 cup) caster sugar

1 teaspoon vanilla extract

1/2 cup desiccated coconut (optional)

METHOD

1. To make the dulce de leche, pour the milk into a heavy-based saucepan and bring to the boil. Add the remaining ingredients and stir until the sugar has completely dissolved. Cook over low-medium heat, stirring occasionally, for 2–3 hours, until reduced to a thick, smooth, tan caramel. To test if your dulce de leche is the right consistency, spoon some onto a plate – if it holds its shape without running, it's ready. Scoop into a bowl and leave to cool.

2. To make the biscuits, put the flours, baking powder and salt in a mixing bowl and combine with your fingers.

3. Add the butter and rub into the flour until the mixture resembles breadcrumbs.

4. Add the sugar and vanilla and mix to a smooth dough. Chill in the refrigerator for 30 minutes.

5. Preheat the oven to 180°C and line some trays with baking paper. Place the dough on a lightly floured work surface and roll out to 1 cm thick. Cut into 5 cm circles with a biscuit cutter and place on the trays.

6. Form the dough off-cuts into a ball, roll out again, and cut more circles. Continue rolling and cutting until you have used all the dough.

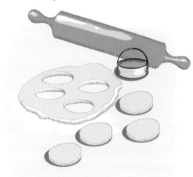

7. Bake the biscuits for 10–15 minutes, until just golden. Transfer to a wire rack to cool completely.

8. Toast the coconut (if using) in a dry frying pan until golden. Transfer to a bowl.

9. Spread the top of a biscuit with dulce de leche and sandwich another biscuit on top. Roll the sides in toasted coconut (if using) – it should stick to the dulce de leche. Continue sandwiching the remaining biscuits with dulce de leche and rolling in coconut. Store the biscuits in a jar.

Tips and tricks

WEIGHTS AND MEASURES

Here is a handy conversion chart that you can use to measure out your ingredients. For dry ingredients, such as dried fruits or nuts, it is usually more accurate to use a scale to measure the weight.

1/2 teaspoon	2.5 ml	2/3 cup	160 ml
1 teaspoon	5 ml	3/4 cup	180 ml
1 tablespoon	20 ml	1 cup	250 ml
1/4 cup	60 ml	2 cups	500 ml
1/3 cup	80 ml	3 cups	750 ml
1/2 cup	125 ml		

SOME HEALTHY HINTS

Always wash your hands with warm, soapy water before and after handling food. You may need to wash your hands several times as you prepare a dish, particularly if you are using raw meat, chicken or fish.

Try not to use the same spoon for cooking and tasting!

Wash all fruits and vegetables in cold water before using them.

Keep your preparation surfaces clean. Scrub all your equipment and chopping boards with hot, soapy water before putting them away.

Handle knives and sharp instruments with care. Always have an adult present when using anything sharp.

Use oven mitts when taking food out of the oven, and always have help around when handling anything hot.

Wear closed-toed shoes in case of spills or breakages.

Get permission before beginning to cook, or before serving food, particularly to young children. Food allergies can be very serious, so make sure an adult is aware of what you are preparing.

Always store foods properly and at the correct temperature. Read the labels on packaging or ask for advice if you are unsure.

Tie long hair back, and make sure your sleeves are rolled up and out of the way. Take off any loose jewellery before you begin cooking — no one wants to find anything other than food in their dinner!

Menu planner

Here is a handy guide that you can use to plan your meal. Photocopy this page and use it to create a special international treat for your family or friends.

STARTER

. . . .

. . . .

. . . .

MAIN

. . . .

. . . .

. . . .

DESSERT

. . . .

. . . .

. . . .

COUNTRY

. . . .

COUNTRY

. . . .

COUNTRY

. . . .

SHOPPING LIST

. . . .

. . . .

. . . .

. . . .

. . . .

. . . .

. . . .

. . . .

. . . .

. . . .

. . . .

Index